THIS PLANNER
BELONGS TO

_____

2018
16-MONTH
WEEKLY PLANNER

A
LITTLE
GOD
TIME

BELLE
CITY
GIFTS

SEPTEMBER 2017

S	M	T	W	T	F	S
					1	2
3	4	5	6	7	8	9
10	11	12	13	14	15	16
17	18	19	20	21	22	23
24	25	26	27	28	29	30

OCTOBER 2017

S	M	T	W	T	F	S
1	2	3	4	5	6	7
8	9	10	11	12	13	14
15	16	17	18	19	20	21
22	23	24	25	26	27	28
29	30	31				

NOVEMBER 2017

S	M	T	W	T	F	S
			1	2	3	4
5	6	7	8	9	10	11
12	13	14	15	16	17	18
19	20	21	22	23	24	25
26	27	28	29	30		

DECEMBER 2017

S	M	T	W	T	F	S
					1	2
3	4	5	6	7	8	9
10	11	12	13	14	15	16
17	18	19	20	21	22	23
24	25	26	27	28	29	30
31						

JANUARY 2018

S	M	T	W	T	F	S
	1	2	3	4	5	6
7	8	9	10	11	12	13
14	15	16	17	18	19	20
21	22	23	24	25	26	27
28	29	30	31			

FEBRUARY 2018

S	M	T	W	T	F	S
				1	2	3
4	5	6	7	8	9	10
11	12	13	14	15	16	17
18	19	20	21	22	23	24
25	26	27	28			

MARCH 2018

S	M	T	W	T	F	S
				1	2	3
4	5	6	7	8	9	10
11	12	13	14	15	16	17
18	19	20	21	22	23	24
25	26	27	28	29	30	31

APRIL 2018

S	M	T	W	T	F	S
1	2	3	4	5	6	7
8	9	10	11	12	13	14
15	16	17	18	19	20	21
22	23	24	25	26	27	28
29	30					

MAY 2018

S	M	T	W	T	F	S
		1	2	3	4	5
6	7	8	9	10	11	12
13	14	15	16	17	18	19
20	21	22	23	24	25	26
27	28	29	30	31		

JUNE 2018

S	M	T	W	T	F	S
					1	2
3	4	5	6	7	8	9
10	11	12	13	14	15	16
17	18	19	20	21	22	23
24	25	26	27	28	29	30

JULY 2018

S	M	T	W	T	F	S
1	2	3	4	5	6	7
8	9	10	11	12	13	14
15	16	17	18	19	20	21
22	23	24	25	26	27	28
29	30	31				

AUGUST 2018

S	M	T	W	T	F	S
			1	2	3	4
5	6	7	8	9	10	11
12	13	14	15	16	17	18
19	20	21	22	23	24	25
26	27	28	29	30	31	

SEPTEMBER 2018

S	M	T	W	T	F	S
						1
2	3	4	5	6	7	8
9	10	11	12	13	14	15
16	17	18	19	20	21	22
23	24	25	26	27	28	29
30						

OCTOBER 2018

S	M	T	W	T	F	S
	1	2	3	4	5	6
7	8	9	10	11	12	13
14	15	16	17	18	19	20
21	22	23	24	25	26	27
28	29	30	31			

NOVEMBER 2018

S	M	T	W	T	F	S
				1	2	3
4	5	6	7	8	9	10
11	12	13	14	15	16	17
18	19	20	21	22	23	24
25	26	27	28	29	30	

DECEMBER 2018

S	M	T	W	T	F	S
						1
2	3	4	5	6	7	8
9	10	11	12	13	14	15
16	17	18	19	20	21	22
23	24	25	26	27	28	29
30	31					

INTRODUCTION

Having trouble fitting everything in your day? This 16-month planner makes getting organized simple and inspiring.

Each beautifully designed page blends practical weekly plans with motivating Scripture. High-quality paper allows you to confidently write reminders, schedules, and personal notes in the space provided.

Stay organized, and be refreshed and inspired as you make *A Little God Time* part of your day.

SEPTEMBER

2017

One thing I have desired of the LORD,

That will I seek:

That I may dwell in the house of the LORD

All the days of my life,

To behold the beauty of the LORD

And to inquire in His temple.

PSALM 27:4 NKJV

S	M	T	W	T	F	S
					1	2
3	4	5	6	7	8	9
10	11	12	13	14	15	16
17	18	19	20	21	22	23
24	25	26	27	28	29	30

AUGUST/SEPTEMBER

28 Monday

_____
_____
_____
_____
_____

29 Tuesday

_____
_____
_____
_____
_____

30 Wednesday

_____
_____
_____
_____
_____

Thursday 31

_____

_____

_____

_____

_____

Friday 1

_____

_____

_____

_____

_____

Saturday 2

_____

_____

_____

Sunday 3

_____

_____

_____

THE LORD WILL GIVE STRENGTH TO HIS PEOPLE;
THE LORD WILL BLESS HIS PEOPLE WITH PEACE.

Psalm 29:11 NKJV

SEPTEMBER

4   Monday   LABOR DAY

_____
_____
_____
_____
_____

5   Tuesday

_____
_____
_____
_____
_____

6   Wednesday

_____
_____
_____
_____
_____

Thursday 7

Friday 8

Saturday 9

Sunday 10

BLESSED IS ANYONE WHO ENDURES TEMPTATION.
SUCH A ONE HAS STOOD THE TEST AND WILL RECEIVE
THE CROWN OF LIFE THAT THE LORD HAS PROMISED
TO THOSE WHO LOVE HIM.

James 1:12 NRSV

SEPTEMBER

11 Monday

_____
_____
_____
_____
_____

12 Tuesday

_____
_____
_____
_____
_____

13 Wednesday

_____
_____
_____
_____
_____

Thursday 14

_____

_____

_____

_____

_____

Friday 15

_____

_____

_____

_____

_____

Saturday 16

_____

_____

_____

Sunday 17

_____

_____

_____

MY VOICE YOU SHALL HEAR IN THE MORNING, O LORD;
IN THE MORNING I WILL DIRECT IT TO YOU,
AND I WILL LOOK UP.

PSALM 5:3 NKJV

SEPTEMBER

18 Monday

_____
_____
_____
_____
_____

19 Tuesday

_____
_____
_____
_____
_____

20 Wednesday   ROSH HASHANAH BEGINS

_____
_____
_____
_____
_____

Thursday 21

_____

_____

_____

_____

_____

AUTUMNAL EQUINOX / ROSH HASHANAH ENDS **Friday 22**

_____

_____

_____

_____

_____

Saturday 23

_____

_____

_____

Sunday 24

_____

_____

_____

THE LORD ALWAYS KEEPS HIS PROMISES;
HE IS GRACIOUS IN ALL HE DOES.

Psalm 145:13 NLT

SEPTEMBER/OCTOBER

25 Monday

_____
_____
_____
_____
_____

26 Tuesday

_____
_____
_____
_____
_____

27 Wednesday

_____
_____
_____
_____
_____

Thursday 28

YOM KIPPUR BEGINS Friday 29

YOM KIPPUR ENDS Saturday 30

Sunday 1

YOUR PROMISES HAVE BEEN THOROUGHLY TESTED,
AND YOUR SERVANT LOVES THEM.

Psalm 119:40 NIV

OCTOBER

2017

Be truly glad! There is wonderful joy ahead.... You love him even though you have never seen him. Though you do not see him now, you trust him; and you rejoice with a glorious, inexpressible joy.

1 PETER 1:6, 8–9 NLT

S	M	T	W	T	F	S
1	2	3	4	5	6	7
8	9	10	11	12	13	14
15	16	17	18	19	20	21
22	23	24	25	26	27	28
29	30	31				

OCTOBER

2 Monday
_____
_____
_____
_____

3 Tuesday
_____
_____
_____
_____

4 Wednesday
_____
_____
_____
_____
_____

Thursday 5

_____

_____

_____

_____

Friday 6

_____

_____

_____

_____

Saturday 7

_____

_____

Sunday 8

_____

_____

_____

THE DESIRES OF THE DILIGENT ARE FULLY SATISFIED.

Proverbs 13:4 NIV

OCTOBER

9   **Monday**   COLUMBUS DAY

_____

_____

_____

_____

_____

10   Tuesday

_____

_____

_____

_____

_____

11   Wednesday

_____

_____

_____

_____

_____

Thursday 12

Friday 13

Saturday 14

Sunday 15

HE WILL GIVE ETERNAL LIFE TO THOSE WHO
KEEP ON DOING GOOD,
SEEKING AFTER THE GLORY AND HONOR AND
IMMORTALITY THAT GOD OFFERS.

Romans 2:7 NLT

OCTOBER

16 Monday

_____
_____
_____
_____

17 Tuesday

_____
_____
_____
_____

18 Wednesday

_____
_____
_____
_____

Thursday 19

Friday 20

Saturday 21

Sunday 22

MY FLESH AND MY HEART MAY FAIL,
BUT GOD IS THE STRENGTH OF MY HEART
AND MY PORTION FOREVER.

Psalm 73:26 NIV

OCTOBER

23 Monday

_____
_____
_____
_____

24 Tuesday

_____
_____
_____
_____

25 Wednesday

_____
_____
_____
_____

Thursday 26

_____

_____

_____

_____

Friday 27

_____

_____

_____

_____

Saturday 28

_____

_____

Sunday 29

_____

_____

_____

For you who fear my name,
the sun of righteousness shall rise
with healing in its wings.

Malachi 4:2 ESV

NOVEMBER
2017

Praise the LORD!

Praise God in his sanctuary;

praise him in his mighty heavens!

Praise him for his mighty deeds;

praise him according to his excellent greatness!

Let everything that has breath praise the LORD!

Praise the LORD!

PSALM 150:1-2, 6 ESV

S	M	T	W	T	F	S
			1	2	3	4
5	6	7	8	9	10	11
12	13	14	15	16	17	18
19	20	21	22	23	24	25
26	27	28	29	30		

OCTOBER/NOVEMBER

30 Monday

_____
_____
_____
_____
_____

31 Tuesday

_____
_____
_____
_____
_____

1 Wednesday

_____
_____
_____
_____
_____

Thursday 2

_____

_____

_____

_____

_____

Friday 3

_____

_____

_____

_____

_____

Saturday 4

_____

_____

_____

DAYLIGHT SAVING TIME ENDS Sunday 5

_____

_____

_____

THOSE WHO KNOW YOUR NAME WILL PUT THEIR TRUST IN YOU;
FOR YOU, LORD, HAVE NOT FORSAKEN THOSE WHO SEEK YOU.

Psalm 9:10 NKJV

NOVEMBER

6 Monday

_____
_____
_____
_____
_____

7 Tuesday   ELECTION DAY

_____
_____
_____
_____
_____

8 Wednesday

_____
_____
_____
_____
_____

Thursday 9

_____

_____

_____

_____

_____

Friday 10

_____

_____

_____

_____

_____

VETERANS' DAY Saturday 11

_____

_____

_____

Sunday 12

_____

_____

_____

I TRUST IN YOU, O LORD;
I SAY, "YOU ARE MY GOD."
MY TIMES ARE IN YOUR HAND.

Psalm 31:14-15 ESV

NOVEMBER

13 Monday

_____
_____
_____
_____
_____

14 Tuesday

_____
_____
_____
_____
_____

15 Wednesday

_____
_____
_____
_____
_____

Thursday 16

Friday 17

Saturday 18

Sunday 19

THE LAW OF THE LORD IS PERFECT,
REFRESHING THE SOUL.

Psalm 19:7 NIV

NOVEMBER

20 Monday

_____
_____
_____
_____
_____

21 Tuesday

_____
_____
_____
_____
_____

22 Wednesday

_____
_____
_____
_____
_____

_____
_____
_____
_____
_____

Friday 24

_____
_____
_____
_____
_____

Saturday 25

_____
_____
_____

Sunday 26

_____
_____
_____

YOU WERE CLEANSED FROM YOUR SINS WHEN YOU OBEYED THE TRUTH.

1 Peter 1:22 NLT

NOVEMBER/DECEMBER

27 Monday

_____
_____
_____
_____
_____

28 Tuesday

_____
_____
_____
_____
_____

29 Wednesday

_____
_____
_____
_____
_____

Thursday 30

_____

_____

_____

_____

_____

Friday 1

_____

_____

_____

_____

_____

Saturday 2

_____

_____

_____

Sunday 3

_____

_____

_____

DO NOT LET WISDOM AND UNDERSTANDING OUT OF YOUR SIGHT,
PRESERVE SOUND JUDGMENT AND DISCRETION;
THEY WILL BE LIFE FOR YOU.

Proverbs 3:21-22 NIV

DECEMBER

2017

O Lord, You have searched me and known me.

You know my sitting down and my rising up;

You understand my thought afar off.

You comprehend my path and my lying down,

And are acquainted with all my ways.

For there is not a word on my tongue,

But behold, O Lord, You know it altogether.

PSALM 139:1-4 NKJV

S	M	T	W	T	F	S
					1	2
3	4	5	6	7	8	9
10	11	12	13	14	15	16
17	18	19	20	21	22	23
24	25	26	27	28	29	30
31						

DECEMBER

4   Monday

_____
_____
_____
_____
_____

5   Tuesday

_____
_____
_____
_____
_____

6   Wednesday

_____
_____
_____
_____
_____

Thursday 7

_____
_____
_____
_____
_____

Friday 8

_____
_____
_____
_____
_____

Saturday 9

_____
_____
_____

Sunday 10

_____
_____
_____

The Lord gives wisdom;
from his mouth come knowledge and understanding.

Proverbs 2:6-7 ESV

DECEMBER

11 Monday

_____
_____
_____
_____

12 Tuesday   FIRST DAY OF HANUKKAH

_____
_____
_____
_____

13 Wednesday

_____
_____
_____
_____
_____

Thursday 14

_____
_____
_____
_____
_____

Friday 15

_____
_____
_____
_____
_____

Saturday 16

_____
_____
_____

Sunday 17

_____
_____
_____

THE WISDOM FROM ABOVE IS FIRST OF ALL PURE.
IT IS ALSO PEACE LOVING, GENTLE AT ALL TIMES,
AND WILLING TO YIELD TO OTHERS.
IT IS FULL OF MERCY AND GOOD DEEDS.
IT SHOWS NO FAVORITISM AND IS ALWAYS SINCERE.

James 3:17 NLT

DECEMBER

18 Monday

_____
_____
_____
_____
_____

19 Tuesday

_____
_____
_____
_____

20 Wednesday   LAST DAY OF HANUKKAH

_____
_____
_____
_____
_____

Friday 22

Saturday 23

CHRISTMAS EVE **Sunday** 24

YOU WILL EXPERIENCE GOD'S PEACE,
WHICH EXCEEDS ANYTHING WE CAN UNDERSTAND.
HIS PEACE WILL GUARD YOUR HEARTS AND MINDS
AS YOU LIVE IN CHRIST JESUS.

Philippians 4:7 NLT

DECEMBER

25 Monday CHRISTMAS DAY

_____
_____
_____
_____

26 Tuesday

_____
_____
_____
_____

27 Wednesday

_____
_____
_____
_____

Thursday 28

Friday 29

Saturday 30

Sunday 31

HE WHO HAS CLEAN HANDS AND A PURE HEART,
WHO HAS NOT LIFTED UP HIS SOUL TO FALSEHOOD
AND HAS NOT SWORN DECEITFULLY.
HE SHALL RECEIVE A BLESSING FROM THE LORD
AND RIGHTEOUSNESS FROM THE GOD OF HIS SALVATION.

Psalm 24:5 NASB

JANUARY
2018

God has said,

"I will never fail you.

I will never abandon you."

So we can say with confidence,

"The LORD is my helper,

so I will have no fear."

HEBREWS 13:5-6 NLT

S	M	T	W	T	F	S
	1	2	3	4	5	6
7	8	9	10	11	12	13
14	15	16	17	18	19	20
21	22	23	24	25	26	27
28	29	30	31			

JANUARY

1   Monday   NEW YEAR'S DAY

_____
_____
_____
_____
_____

2   Tuesday

_____
_____
_____
_____
_____

3   Wednesday

_____
_____
_____
_____
_____

Thursday 4

_____

_____

_____

_____

_____

Friday 5

_____

_____

_____

_____

_____

Saturday 6

_____

_____

_____

Sunday 7

_____

_____

_____

THE LORD LOVES JUSTICE AND FAIRNESS;
HE WILL NEVER ABANDON HIS PEOPLE.
THEY WILL BE KEPT SAFE FOREVER.

Psalm 37:28 TLB

JANUARY

8 Monday

_____
_____
_____
_____
_____

9 Tuesday

_____
_____
_____
_____
_____

10 Wednesday

_____
_____
_____
_____
_____

Thursday 11

_____

_____

_____

_____

Friday 12

_____

_____

_____

_____

_____

Saturday 13

_____

_____

_____

Sunday 14

_____

_____

_____

THE LORD HEARS HIS PEOPLE WHEN THEY CALL TO HIM FOR HELP.
HE RESCUES THEM FROM ALL THEIR TROUBLES.

Psalm 34:17 NLT

JANUARY

15   **Monday**   MARTIN LUTHER KING DAY

_____
_____
_____
_____
_____

16   **Tuesday**

_____
_____
_____
_____
_____

17   **Wednesday**

_____
_____
_____
_____
_____

Thursday 18

Friday 19

Saturday 20

Sunday 21

IF GOD IS FOR US, WHO CAN BE AGAINST US?

Romans 8:31 ESV

JANUARY

22 Monday

_____
_____
_____
_____
_____

23 Tuesday

_____
_____
_____
_____
_____

24 Wednesday

_____
_____
_____
_____
_____

Thursday 25

_____
_____
_____
_____

Friday 26

_____
_____
_____
_____
_____

Saturday 27

_____
_____
_____

Sunday 28

_____
_____
_____

SUBMIT TO GOD. RESIST THE DEVIL AND HE WILL FLEE FROM YOU.

James 4:7 NKJV

FEBRUARY

2018

*Take delight in the L*ORD*,*

and he will give you your heart's desires.

*Commit everything you do to the L*ORD*.*

Trust him, and he will help you.

PSALM 37:4-5 NLT

S	M	T	W	T	F	S
				1	2	3
4	5	6	7	8	9	10
11	12	13	14	15	16	17
18	19	20	21	22	23	24
25	26	27	28			

JANUARY/FEBRUARY

29 Monday

_____
_____
_____
_____

30 Tuesday

_____
_____
_____
_____

31 Wednesday

_____
_____
_____
_____
_____

Thursday 1

GROUNDHOG DAY Friday 2

Saturday 3

Sunday 4

THOSE WITH GOOD SENSE ARE SLOW TO ANGER,
AND IT IS THEIR GLORY TO OVERLOOK AN OFFENSE.

Proverbs 19:11 NRSV

FEBRUARY

5   Monday

_____
_____
_____
_____
_____

6   Tuesday

_____
_____
_____
_____
_____

7   Wednesday

_____
_____
_____
_____
_____

Thursday 8

_____

_____

_____

_____

Friday 9

_____

_____

_____

_____

Saturday 10

_____

_____

Sunday 11

_____

_____

_____

YOU KEEP HIM IN PERFECT PEACE
WHOSE MIND IS STAYED ON YOU,
BECAUSE HE TRUSTS IN YOU.

Isaiah 26:3 ESV

FEBRUARY

12 Monday

_____
_____
_____
_____

13 Tuesday

_____
_____
_____
_____

14 Wednesday   VALENTINE'S DAY / ASH WEDNESDAY

_____
_____
_____
_____
_____

Thursday 15

_____

_____

_____

_____

Friday 16

_____

_____

_____

_____

Saturday 17

_____

_____

Sunday 18

_____

_____

_____

"BLESSED ARE THOSE WHO HAVE NOT SEEN AND YET HAVE BELIEVED."

John 20:29 ESV

FEBRUARY

19 Monday   PRESIDENTS' DAY

_____
_____
_____
_____
_____

20 Tuesday

_____
_____
_____
_____
_____

21 Wednesday

_____
_____
_____
_____
_____

Thursday 22

_____

_____

_____

_____

_____

Friday 23

_____

_____

_____

_____

Saturday 24

_____

_____

_____

Sunday 25

_____

_____

_____

SURELY YOU HAVE GRANTED HIM UNENDING BLESSINGS
AND MADE HIM GLAD WITH THE JOY OF YOUR PRESENCE.

Psalm 21:6 NIV

FEBRUARY/MARCH

26 Monday

_____
_____
_____
_____
_____

27 Tuesday

_____
_____
_____
_____
_____

28 Wednesday

_____
_____
_____
_____
_____

Thursday 1

Friday 2

Saturday 3

Sunday 4

RELIGION THAT IS PURE AND UNDEFILED BEFORE GOD,
THE FATHER, IS THIS: TO CARE FOR ORPHANS AND WIDOWS IN
THEIR DISTRESS, AND TO KEEP ONESELF UNSTAINED BY THE WORLD.

James 1:27 NRSV

MARCH

2018

Blessed be the God and Father of our Lord Jesus Christ, who has blessed us in Christ with every spiritual blessing in the heavenly places, even as he chose us in him before the foundation of the world, that we should be holy and blameless before him.

EPHESIANS 1:3-4 ESV

S	M	T	W	T	F	S
				1	2	3
4	5	6	7	8	9	10
11	12	13	14	15	16	17
18	19	20	21	22	23	24
25	26	27	28	29	30	31

MARCH

5   Monday

_____

_____

_____

_____

_____

6   Tuesday

_____

_____

_____

_____

_____

7   Wednesday

_____

_____

_____

_____

_____

Thursday 8

Friday 9

Saturday 10

Sunday 11

EVERY GOOD GIFT AND EVERY PERFECT GIFT IS FROM ABOVE,
COMING DOWN FROM THE FATHER OF LIGHTS WITH WHOM THERE
IS NO VARIATION OR SHADOW DUE TO CHANGE.

James 1:17 ESV

MARCH

12 Monday

_____
_____
_____
_____
_____

13 Tuesday

_____
_____
_____
_____
_____

14 Wednesday

_____
_____
_____
_____
_____

Thursday 15

_____

_____

_____

_____

_____

Friday 16

_____

_____

_____

_____

_____

ST. PATRICK'S DAY Saturday 17

_____

_____

_____

Sunday 18

_____

_____

_____

"SEEK FIRST THE KINGDOM OF GOD AND HIS RIGHTEOUSNESS,
AND ALL THESE THINGS SHALL BE ADDED TO YOU."

Matthew 6:33 NKJV

MARCH

19 Monday

_____
_____
_____
_____
_____

20 Tuesday   SPRING EQUINOX

_____
_____
_____
_____
_____

21 Wednesday

_____
_____
_____
_____
_____

Thursday 22

Friday 23

Saturday 24

Sunday 25

THE LORD LONGS TO BE GRACIOUS TO YOU;
THEREFORE HE WILL RISE UP TO SHOW YOU COMPASSION.
FOR THE LORD IS A GOD OF JUSTICE.
BLESSED ARE ALL WHO WAIT FOR HIM!

Isaiah 30:18 NIV

MARCH/APRIL

26 Monday

_____
_____
_____
_____
_____

27 Tuesday

_____
_____
_____
_____
_____

28 Wednesday

_____
_____
_____
_____
_____

Thursday 29

FIRST DAY OF PASSOVER / GOOD FRIDAY Friday 30

Saturday 31

EASTER SUNDAY Sunday 1

I CAN DO EVERYTHING THROUGH CHRIST, WHO GIVES ME STRENGTH.

Philippians 4:13 NLT

APRIL

2018

I will sing of the LORD's great love forever;

with my mouth I will make your faithfulness

known through all generations.

I will declare that your

love stands firm forever,

that you have established

your faithfulness in heaven itself.

PSALM 89:1-2 NIV

S	M	T	W	T	F	S
1	2	3	4	5	6	7
8	9	10	11	12	13	14
15	16	17	18	19	20	21
22	23	24	25	26	27	28
29	30					

APRIL

2   Monday

_____
_____
_____
_____

3   Tuesday

_____
_____
_____
_____

4   Wednesday

_____
_____
_____
_____

Thursday 5

Friday 6

Saturday 7

Sunday 8

LET US THEN APPROACH GOD'S THRONE OF GRACE
WITH CONFIDENCE, SO THAT WE MAY RECEIVE MERCY
AND FIND GRACE TO HELP US IN OUR TIME OF NEED.

Hebrews 4:16 NIV

APRIL

9   Monday

_____
_____
_____
_____
_____

10   Tuesday

_____
_____
_____
_____
_____

11   Wednesday

_____
_____
_____
_____
_____

Thursday 12

_____

_____

_____

_____

_____

Friday 13

_____

_____

_____

_____

_____

Saturday 14

_____

_____

_____

Sunday 15

_____

_____

_____

WE ARE GOD'S MASTERPIECE. HE HAS CREATED US
ANEW IN CHRIST JESUS, SO WE CAN DO THE GOOD
THINGS HE PLANNED FOR US LONG AGO.

Ephesians 2:10 NLT

APRIL

16 Monday

_____
_____
_____
_____
_____

17 Tuesday

_____
_____
_____
_____
_____

18 Wednesday

_____
_____
_____
_____
_____

Thursday 19

_____
_____
_____
_____

Friday 20

_____
_____
_____
_____

Saturday 21

_____
_____
_____

Sunday 22

_____
_____
_____

BE OF THE SAME MIND TOWARD ONE ANOTHER. DO NOT
SET YOUR MIND ON HIGH THINGS, BUT ASSOCIATE WITH
THE HUMBLE. DO NOT BE WISE IN YOUR OWN OPINION.

Romans 12:16 NKJV

APRIL

23 Monday

_____
_____
_____
_____

24 Tuesday

_____
_____
_____
_____

25 Wednesday

_____
_____
_____
_____

Thursday 26

_____

_____

_____

_____

Friday 27

_____

_____

_____

_____

Saturday 28

_____

_____

Sunday 29

_____

_____

_____

BE STRONG AND COURAGEOUS. DO NOT BE
FRIGHTENED, AND DO NOT BE DISMAYED, FOR THE
LORD YOUR GOD IS WITH YOU WHEREVER YOU GO.

Joshua 1:9 ESV

MAY
2018

Be my rock of refuge,

to which I can always go;

give the command to save me,

for you are my rock and my fortress....

You have been my hope, Sovereign LORD,

my confidence since my youth.

PSALM 71:3, 5 NIV

S	M	T	W	T	F	S
		1	2	3	4	5
6	7	8	9	10	11	12
13	14	15	16	17	18	19
20	21	22	23	24	25	26
27	28	29	30	31		

MAY

30 Monday

_____
_____
_____
_____
_____

1 Tuesday

_____
_____
_____
_____
_____

2 Wednesday

_____
_____
_____
_____
_____

Friday 4

Saturday 5

Sunday 6

THE WHOLE EARTH IS FILLED WITH AWE AT YOUR WONDERS.

Psalm 65:8 NIV

MAY

7 Monday

_____
_____
_____
_____

8 Tuesday

_____
_____
_____
_____
_____

9 Wednesday

_____
_____
_____
_____
_____

Thursday 10

Friday 11

Saturday 12

MOTHER'S DAY **Sunday** 13

WHY AM I SO SAD?
WHY AM I SO UPSET?
I SHOULD PUT MY HOPE IN GOD
AND KEEP PRAISING HIM.

Psalm 42:11 NCV

MAY

14 Monday

_____
_____
_____
_____
_____

15 Tuesday

_____
_____
_____
_____
_____

16 Wednesday

_____
_____
_____
_____
_____

Thursday 17

Friday 18

Saturday 19

PENTECOST Sunday 20

Take a new grip with your tired hands and strengthen your weak knees. Mark out a straight path for your feet so that those who are weak and lame will not fall but become strong.

Hebrews 12:12-14 NLT

MAY

21 Monday

_____
_____
_____
_____

22 Tuesday

_____
_____
_____
_____

23 Wednesday

_____
_____
_____
_____
_____

Thursday 24

_____

_____

_____

_____

Friday 25

_____

_____

_____

_____

Saturday 26

_____

_____

Sunday 27

_____

_____

WHOEVER PURSUES RIGHTEOUSNESS AND LOVE FINDS LIFE,
PROSPERITY AND HONOR.

Proverbs 21:21 NIV

MAY/JUNE

28 Monday   MEMORIAL DAY

_____
_____
_____
_____
_____

29 Tuesday

_____
_____
_____
_____
_____

30 Wednesday

_____
_____
_____
_____
_____

Thursday 31

_____

_____

_____

_____

Friday 1

_____

_____

_____

_____

Saturday 2

_____

_____

_____

Sunday 3

_____

_____

_____

LET US NOT NEGLECT OUR MEETING TOGETHER, AS SOME
PEOPLE DO, BUT ENCOURAGE ONE ANOTHER, ESPECIALLY
NOW THAT THE DAY OF HIS RETURN IS DRAWING NEAR.

Hebrews 10:25 NLT

JUNE

2018

The LORD your God is in your midst,

a mighty one who will save;

he will rejoice over you with gladness;

he will quiet you by his love;

he will exult over you with loud singing.

ZEPHANIAH 3:17 ESV

S	M	T	W	T	F	S
					1	2
3	4	5	6	7	8	9
10	11	12	13	14	15	16
17	18	19	20	21	22	23
24	25	26	27	28	29	30

JUNE

4 Monday

_____
_____
_____
_____

5 Tuesday

_____
_____
_____
_____

6 Wednesday

_____
_____
_____
_____
_____

Thursday 7

_____

_____

_____

_____

_____

Friday 8

_____

_____

_____

_____

_____

Saturday 9

_____

_____

_____

Sunday 10

_____

_____

_____

DO YOUR BEST TO PRESENT YOURSELF TO GOD AS ONE
APPROVED BY HIM, A WORKER WHO HAS NO NEED TO BE
ASHAMED, RIGHTLY EXPLAINING THE WORD OF TRUTH.

2 Timothy 2:15 NRSV

JUNE

11 Monday

_____
_____
_____
_____

12 Tuesday

_____
_____
_____
_____

13 Wednesday

_____
_____
_____
_____
_____

_____

_____

_____

_____

_____

Friday 15

_____

_____

_____

_____

_____

Saturday 16

_____

_____

_____

FATHER'S DAY **Sunday** 17

_____

_____

_____

"I WILL COME BACK AND TAKE YOU TO BE WITH
ME THAT YOU ALSO MAY BE WHERE I AM."

John 14:3 NIV

JUNE

18 Monday

_____
_____
_____
_____

19 Tuesday

_____
_____
_____
_____

20 Wednesday

_____
_____
_____
_____

_____

_____

_____

_____

_____

Friday 22

_____

_____

_____

_____

_____

Saturday 23

_____

_____

_____

Sunday 24

_____

_____

_____

"IF YOU HAVE FAITH LIKE A GRAIN OF MUSTARD SEED, YOU WILL SAY
TO THIS MOUNTAIN, 'MOVE FROM HERE TO THERE,' AND IT WILL
MOVE, AND NOTHING WILL BE IMPOSSIBLE FOR YOU."

Matthew 17:20 ESV

JUNE

25 Monday

_____
_____
_____
_____
_____

26 Tuesday

_____
_____
_____
_____
_____

27 Wednesday

_____
_____
_____
_____
_____

Thursday 28

_____

_____

_____

_____

Friday 29

_____

_____

_____

_____

Saturday 30

_____

_____

_____

Sunday 1

_____

_____

_____

WHETHER YOU EAT OR DRINK,
OR WHATEVER YOU DO, DO ALL TO THE GLORY OF GOD.

1 Corinthians 10:31 NKJV

JULY
2018

You created my inmost being;

you knit me together in my mother's womb.

I praise you because I am fearfully

and wonderfully made;

your works are wonderful,

I know that full well.

PSALM 139:13-14 NIV

S	M	T	W	T	F	S
1	2	3	4	5	6	7
8	9	10	11	12	13	14
15	16	17	18	19	20	21
22	23	24	25	26	27	28
29	30	31				

JULY

2 Monday

_____
_____
_____
_____
_____

3 Tuesday

_____
_____
_____
_____
_____

4 Wednesday   INDEPENDENCE DAY

_____
_____
_____
_____
_____
_____

Thursday 5

Friday 6

Saturday 7

Sunday 8

WITHOUT FAITH IT IS IMPOSSIBLE TO PLEASE GOD, BECAUSE
ANYONE WHO COMES TO HIM MUST BELIEVE THAT HE EXISTS
AND THAT HE REWARDS THOSE WHO EARNESTLY SEEK HIM.

Hebrews 11:6 NIV

JULY

9 Monday

_____
_____
_____
_____
_____

10 Tuesday

_____
_____
_____
_____
_____

11 Wednesday

_____
_____
_____
_____
_____

Thursday 12

_____
_____
_____
_____
_____

Friday 13

_____
_____
_____
_____
_____

Saturday 14

_____
_____
_____

Sunday 15

_____
_____
_____

GOD IS FAITHFUL. HE WILL NOT ALLOW THE
TEMPTATION TO BE MORE THAN YOU CAN STAND.
WHEN YOU ARE TEMPTED, HE WILL SHOW YOU A WAY
OUT SO THAT YOU CAN ENDURE.

1 Corinthians 10:13 NLT

JULY

16 Monday

_____
_____
_____
_____

17 Tuesday

_____
_____
_____
_____

18 Wednesday

_____
_____
_____
_____
_____

Thursday 19

_____

_____

_____

_____

Friday 20

_____

_____

_____

_____

Saturday 21

_____

_____

_____

Sunday 22

_____

_____

_____

WHEN YOU LIE DOWN,
YOU WILL NOT BE AFRAID;
WHEN YOU LIE DOWN,
YOUR SLEEP WILL BE SWEET.

Proverbs 3:24 NIV

JULY

23 Monday

_____
_____
_____
_____
_____

24 Tuesday

_____
_____
_____
_____
_____

25 Wednesday

_____
_____
_____
_____
_____

Thursday 26

_____

_____

_____

_____

Friday 27

_____

_____

_____

_____

Saturday 28

_____

_____

Sunday 29

_____

_____

_____

GOD HAS NOT GIVEN US A SPIRIT OF FEAR,
BUT OF POWER AND OF LOVE AND OF A SOUND MIND.

2 Timothy 1:7 NKJV

AUGUST
2018

*Consider it pure joy, my brothers and
sisters, whenever you face trials of many
kinds, because you know that the testing
of your faith produces perseverance.*

JAMES 1:2-3 NIV

S	M	T	W	T	F	S
			1	2	3	4
5	6	7	8	9	10	11
12	13	14	15	16	17	18
19	20	21	22	23	24	25
26	27	28	29	30	31	

JULY/AUGUST

30 Monday

_____
_____
_____
_____
_____

31 Tuesday

_____
_____
_____
_____
_____

1 Wednesday

_____
_____
_____
_____
_____

Thursday   2

Friday   3

Saturday   4

Sunday   5

YOU ARE OUR FATHER;
WE ARE THE CLAY, AND YOU OUR POTTER;
AND ALL WE ARE THE WORK OF YOUR HAND.

Isaiah 64:8 NKJV

AUGUST

6   Monday

_____
_____
_____
_____
_____

7   Tuesday

_____
_____
_____
_____
_____

8   Wednesday

_____
_____
_____
_____
_____

Thursday 9

_____
_____
_____
_____
_____

Friday 10

_____
_____
_____
_____
_____

Saturday 11

_____
_____
_____

Sunday 12

_____
_____
_____

HE IS SO RICH IN KINDNESS AND GRACE THAT
HE PURCHASED OUR FREEDOM WITH THE
BLOOD OF HIS SON AND FORGAVE OUR SINS.

Ephesians 1:7 NLT

AUGUST

13 Monday

_____
_____
_____
_____
_____

14 Tuesday

_____
_____
_____
_____
_____

15 Wednesday

_____
_____
_____
_____
_____

Thursday 16

_____

_____

_____

_____

_____

Friday 17

_____

_____

_____

_____

_____

Saturday 18

_____

_____

_____

Sunday 19

_____

_____

_____

YOU, LORD, ARE GOOD, AND READY TO FORGIVE,
AND ABUNDANT IN MERCY TO ALL THOSE WHO CALL UPON YOU.

Psalm 86:5 NKJV

AUGUST

20 Monday

_____
_____
_____
_____

21 Tuesday

_____
_____
_____
_____

22 Wednesday

_____
_____
_____
_____
_____

Thursday 23

_____

_____

_____

_____

_____

Friday 24

_____

_____

_____

_____

_____

Saturday 25

_____

_____

_____

Sunday 26

_____

_____

_____

WHOEVER IS GENEROUS TO THE POOR LENDS TO THE LORD,
AND HE WILL REPAY HIM FOR HIS DEED.

Proverbs 19:17 ESV

AUGUST/SEPTEMBER

27 Monday

_____
_____
_____
_____
_____

28 Tuesday

_____
_____
_____
_____
_____

29 Wednesday

_____
_____
_____
_____
_____

Thursday 30

_____
_____
_____
_____
_____

Friday 31

_____
_____
_____
_____
_____

Saturday 1

_____
_____
_____

Sunday 2

_____
_____
_____

"BLESSED ARE THE GENTLE, FOR THEY SHALL INHERIT THE EARTH."

Matthew 5:5 NASB

SEPTEMBER

2018

We do not lose heart, but though our outer man is decaying, yet our inner man is being renewed day by day. For momentary, light affliction is producing for us an eternal weight of glory far beyond all comparison.

2 CORINTHIANS 4:16-17 NASB

S	M	T	W	T	F	S
						1
2	3	4	5	6	7	8
9	10	11	12	13	14	15
16	17	18	19	20	21	22
23	24	25	26	27	28	29
30						

SEPTEMBER

3 **Monday** LABOR DAY

_____
_____
_____
_____
_____

4 **Tuesday**

_____
_____
_____
_____
_____

5 **Wednesday**

_____
_____
_____
_____
_____
_____

Thursday 6

_____
_____
_____
_____
_____

Friday 7

_____
_____
_____
_____

Saturday 8

_____
_____
_____

ROSH HASHANAH BEGINS Sunday 9

_____
_____
_____

THE LORD IS GOOD TO ALL,
AND HIS MERCY IS OVER ALL THAT HE HAS MADE.

Psalm 145:9 ESV

SEPTEMBER

10 Monday

_____

_____

_____

_____

11 Tuesday   ROSH HASHANAH ENDS

_____

_____

_____

_____

12 Wednesday

_____

_____

_____

_____

_____

Thursday 13

_____
_____
_____
_____

Friday 14

_____
_____
_____
_____

Saturday 15

_____
_____
_____

Sunday 16

_____
_____
_____

THE RANSOMED OF THE LORD WILL RETURN. THEY WILL
ENTER ZION WITH SINGING; EVERLASTING JOY WILL CROWN
THEIR HEADS. GLADNESS AND JOY WILL OVERTAKE THEM,
AND SORROW AND SIGHING WILL FLEE AWAY.

Isaiah 35:10 NIV

SEPTEMBER

17 Monday

_____
_____
_____
_____
_____

18 Tuesday   YOM KIPPUR BEGINS

_____
_____
_____
_____
_____

19 Wednesday   YOM KIPPUR ENDS

_____
_____
_____
_____
_____

Thursday 20

_____
_____
_____
_____

Friday 21

_____
_____
_____
_____

Saturday 22

_____
_____

AUTUMNAL EQUINOX Sunday 23

_____
_____
_____

I CONSIDER THAT THE SUFFERINGS OF THIS PRESENT TIME ARE NOT
WORTH COMPARING WITH THE GLORY THAT IS TO BE REVEALED TO US.

Romans 8:18 ESV

SEPTEMBER

24 Monday

_____
_____
_____
_____

25 Tuesday

_____
_____
_____
_____
_____

26 Wednesday

_____
_____
_____
_____
_____

Thursday 27

_____
_____
_____
_____
_____

Friday 28

_____
_____
_____
_____
_____

Saturday 29

_____
_____
_____

Sunday 30

_____
_____
_____

WE CAN MAKE OUR PLANS, BUT THE LORD DETERMINES OUR STEPS.

Proverbs 16:9 NLT

OCTOBER
2018

With me are riches and honor,

enduring wealth and prosperity.

My fruit is better than fine gold;

what I yield surpasses choice silver.

I walk in the way of righteousness,

along the paths of justice,

bestowing a rich inheritance

on those who love me

and making their treasuries full.

PROVERBS 8:18-21 NIV

	S	M	T	W	T	F	S
		1	2	3	4	5	6
	7	8	9	10	11	12	13
	14	15	16	17	18	19	20
	21	22	23	24	25	26	27
	28	29	30	31			

OCTOBER

1 Monday

_____
_____
_____
_____
_____

2 Tuesday

_____
_____
_____
_____
_____

3 Wednesday

_____
_____
_____
_____
_____

Thursday 4

_____

_____

_____

_____

Friday 5

_____

_____

_____

_____

Saturday 6

_____

_____

_____

Sunday 7

_____

_____

_____

THOSE WHO DEAL TRUTHFULLY ARE HIS DELIGHT.

Proverbs 12:22 NKJV

OCTOBER

8 Monday COLUMBUS DAY

_____
_____
_____
_____
_____

9 Tuesday

_____
_____
_____
_____
_____

10 Wednesday

_____
_____
_____
_____
_____

Thursday 11

_____
_____
_____
_____

Friday 12

_____
_____
_____
_____

Saturday 13

_____
_____
_____

Sunday 14

_____
_____
_____

"MY FATHER WILL HONOR THE ONE WHO SERVES ME."

John 12:26 NIV

OCTOBER

15 Monday

_____
_____
_____
_____
_____

16 Tuesday

_____
_____
_____
_____
_____

17 Wednesday

_____
_____
_____
_____
_____

Thursday 18

Friday 19

Saturday 20

Sunday 21

THE LORD TAKES PLEASURE IN THOSE WHO FEAR HIM,
IN THOSE WHO HOPE IN HIS MERCY.

Psalm 147:11 NKJV

OCTOBER

22 Monday

_____
_____
_____
_____

23 Tuesday

_____
_____
_____
_____

24 Wednesday

_____
_____
_____
_____

Thursday 25

_____

_____

_____

_____

Friday 26

_____

_____

_____

_____

Saturday 27

_____

_____

_____

Sunday 28

_____

_____

_____

PRIDE WILL RUIN PEOPLE,
BUT THOSE WHO ARE HUMBLE WILL BE HONORED.

Proverbs 29:23 NCV

NOVEMBER
2018

My child, pay attention to what I say.

Listen carefully to my words.

Don't lose sight of them.

Let them penetrate deep into your heart,

for they bring life to those who find them,

and healing to their whole body.

PROVERBS 4:20-22 NLT

S	M	T	W	T	F	S
				1	2	3
4	5	6	7	8	9	10
11	12	13	14	15	16	17
18	19	20	21	22	23	24
25	26	27	28	29	30	

OCTOBER/NOVEMBER

29 Monday

_____
_____
_____
_____

30 Tuesday

_____
_____
_____
_____

31 Wednesday

_____
_____
_____
_____

Thursday 1

_____

_____

_____

_____

_____

Friday 2

_____

_____

_____

_____

_____

Saturday 3

_____

_____

_____

DAYLIGHT SAVING TIME ENDS Sunday 4

_____

_____

_____

YOUR LAWS ARE MY TREASURE;
THEY ARE MY HEART'S DELIGHT.

Psalm 119:111 NLT

NOVEMBER

5   Monday

_____
_____
_____
_____

6   Tuesday   ELECTION DAY

_____
_____
_____
_____

7   Wednesday

_____
_____
_____
_____

Thursday 8

_____

_____

_____

_____

_____

Friday 9

_____

_____

_____

_____

Saturday 10

_____

_____

_____

VETERANS' DAY   Sunday 11

_____

_____

_____

BECAUSE OF MY INTEGRITY YOU UPHOLD ME
AND SET ME IN YOUR PRESENCE FOREVER.

Psalm 41:12 NIV

NOVEMBER

12 Monday

_____
_____
_____
_____

13 Tuesday

_____
_____
_____
_____
_____

14 Wednesday

_____
_____
_____
_____
_____

Thursday 15

_____
_____
_____
_____
_____

Friday 16

_____
_____
_____
_____
_____

Saturday 17

_____
_____
_____

Sunday 18

_____
_____
_____

YOU WILL GO OUT WITH JOY AND BE LED OUT IN PEACE.
THE MOUNTAINS AND HILLS WILL BURST INTO SONG BEFORE YOU,
AND ALL THE TREES IN THE FIELDS WILL CLAP THEIR HANDS.

Isaiah 55:12 NCV

NOVEMBER

19 Monday

_____
_____
_____
_____

20 Tuesday

_____
_____
_____
_____

21 Wednesday

_____
_____
_____
_____

RIGHTEOUSNESS AND JUSTICE ARE
THE FOUNDATION OF YOUR THRONE.

Psalm 89:14 NIV

NOVEMBER/DECEMBER

26 Monday

_____
_____
_____
_____

27 Tuesday

_____
_____
_____
_____
_____

28 Wednesday

_____
_____
_____
_____

Thursday 29

_____

_____

_____

_____

_____

Friday 30

_____

_____

_____

_____

_____

Saturday 1

_____

_____

_____

HANUKKAH BEGINS / FIRST SUNDAY OF ADVENT   Sunday 2

_____

_____

_____

THE LORD IS COMING TO JUDGE THE EARTH.
HE WILL JUDGE THE WORLD WITH JUSTICE,
AND THE NATIONS WITH FAIRNESS.

Psalm 98:9 NLT

DECEMBER

2018

"You are the light of the world. A city set on a hill cannot be hidden. Nor do people light a lamp and put it under a basket, but on a stand, and it gives light to all in the house. In the same way, let your light shine before others, so that they may see your good works and give glory to your Father who is in heaven."

MATTHEW 5:14-16 ESV

S	M	T	W	T	F	S
						1
2	3	4	5	6	7	8
9	10	11	12	13	14	15
16	17	18	19	20	21	22
23	24	25	26	27	28	29
30	31					

DECEMBER

3 Monday

_____
_____
_____
_____
_____

4 Tuesday

_____
_____
_____
_____
_____

5 Wednesday

_____
_____
_____
_____
_____

Thursday 6

_____
_____
_____
_____

Friday 7

_____
_____
_____
_____

Saturday 8

_____
_____
_____

Sunday 9

_____
_____
_____

"LOVE YOUR ENEMIES, AND DO GOOD, AND LEND, EXPECTING
NOTHING IN RETURN, AND YOUR REWARD WILL BE GREAT,
AND YOU WILL BE SONS OF THE MOST HIGH."

Luke 6:35 ESV

DECEMBER

10 Monday HANUKKAH ENDS

_____
_____
_____
_____
_____

11 Tuesday

_____
_____
_____
_____
_____

12 Wednesday

_____
_____
_____
_____
_____

Thursday 13

_____
_____
_____
_____
_____

Friday 14

_____
_____
_____
_____
_____

Saturday 15

_____
_____
_____

Sunday 16

_____
_____
_____

SATISFY US IN THE MORNING WITH YOUR UNFAILING LOVE,
THAT WE MAY SING FOR JOY AND BE GLAD ALL OUR DAYS.

Psalm 90:14 NIV

DECEMBER

17 Monday

_____
_____
_____
_____
_____

18 Tuesday

_____
_____
_____
_____
_____

19 Wednesday

_____
_____
_____
_____
_____

Thursday 20

_____

_____

_____

_____

_____

WINTER SOLSTICE Friday 21

_____

_____

_____

_____

_____

Saturday 22

_____

_____

_____

Sunday 23

_____

_____

_____

THEY WHO WAIT FOR THE LORD SHALL RENEW THEIR
STRENGTH; THEY SHALL MOUNT UP WITH WINGS LIKE EAGLES;
THEY SHALL RUN AND NOT BE WEARY;
THEY SHALL WALK AND NOT FAINT.

Isaiah 40:31 ESV

DECEMBER

24 Monday CHRISTMAS EVE

_____
_____
_____
_____
_____

25 Tuesday CHRISTMAS DAY

_____
_____
_____
_____
_____

26 Wednesday

_____
_____
_____
_____
_____

Thursday 27

_____

_____

_____

_____

Friday 28

_____

_____

_____

_____

Saturday 29

_____

_____

_____

Sunday 30

_____

_____

_____

Monday 31

_____

_____

_____

_____

_____

Belle City Gifts
Racine, Wisconsin, USA

Belle City Gifts is an imprint of BroadStreet Publishing Group LLC.
Broadstreetpublishing.com

A Little God Time 2018 Planner
© 2017 by BroadStreet Publishing

ISBN 978-1-4245-5511-6

Scripture quotations marked (NLT) are taken from the *Holy Bible*, New Living Translation, copyright © 1996,
2004, 2007. Used by permission of Tyndale House Publishers, Inc., Carol Stream, Illinois 60188. All rights
reserved. Scripture quotations marked (NIV) are taken from the Holy Bible, New International Version®,
NIV®. Copyright © 1973, 1978, 1984, 2011 by Biblica, Inc.™ Used by permission of Zondervan. All rights
reserved worldwide. www.zondervan.com. The "NIV" and "New International Version" are trademarks
registered in the United States Patent and Trademark Office by Biblica, Inc.™ Scripture quotations
marked (NCV) are taken from the New Century Version®. Copyright © 2005 by Thomas Nelson. Used by
permission. All rights reserved. Scripture quotations marked (AMP) are taken from the Amplified Bible,
Copyright © 1954, 1958, 1962, 1964, 1965, 1987 by The Lockman Foundation. Used by permission.
Scripture quotations marked (NASB) are taken from the New American Standard Bible®, Copyright © 1960,
1962, 1963, 1968, 1971, 1972, 1973, 1975, 1977, 1995 by The Lockman Foundation. Used by permission.
www.Lockman.org. Scripture quotations marked (NRSV) are taken from the New Revised Standard Version
Bible, copyright 1989, Division of Christian Education of the National Council of the Churches of Christ in
the United States of America. Used by permission. All rights reserved. Scripture quotations marked (ESV)
are from the ESV® Bible (The Holy Bible, English Standard Version®), copyright © 2001 by Crossway, a
publishing ministry of Good News Publishers. Used by permission. All rights reserved. Scripture quotations
marked (TLB) are taken from The Living Bible copyright © 1971. Used by permission of Tyndale House
Publishers, Inc., Carol Stream, Illinois 60188. All rights reserved. Scripture quotations marked (NKJV) are
taken from the New King James Version®. Copyright © 1982 by Thomas Nelson. Used by permission. All
rights reserved.

Design by Garborg Design Works I garborgdesign.com
Compiled and edited by Michelle Winger I literallyprecise.com

Printed in China.

17 18 19 20 21 22 23   7   6   5   4   3   2   1